City Guide to Bishkek

Stephen Stocks

CONTENTS

Foreword   1

About this guide   3

Getting to know Bishkek   5

Part 1 - The great markets of Bishkek   8

Part 2 - Exploring Chuy Avenue   14

Part 3 - Places of worship   40

Part 4 - Day trips out of Bishkek   43

Part 5 - Preparing for your visit   53

Foreword

Kyrgyzstan is a country in which tourism is undoubtedly in its infancy. Home to stunning and relatively unexplored mountain ranges, such as the Pamirs and the Tian Shan, and pristine alpine lakes, many visitors come to enjoy hiking and climbing. Others pass through the country as part of a multi-country Central Asian tour. Whatever their reason for visiting, people often skip over **Bishkek**, the capital city. They use it as an unavoidable transit on the way elsewhere, or as a convenient place just to pick up a visa to some onward destination.

They are quick to leave due to guidebooks and other travel publications focusing on the natural wonders of the country and skipping over Bishkek quite dismissively as a grey, featureless city. Bishkek doesn't get the appreciation it deserves, and that's a pity. The reality is that Bishkek is a wonderfully green and leafy city, with a permanently snow-capped backdrop of the Ala-Too mountain range. It has a strong Soviet flavour, with the many buildings from that era lending an unforgettable atmosphere. Bishkek has a cosy, community air about it, with no towering impersonal skyscrapers, but rather low-rise communities interspersed with local shops, markets and yet more parks. The ravages of globalisation have mostly bypassed the city, and the ubiquitous Starbucks and McDonalds and such like are mercifully absent.

While Kyrgyzstan and its neighbours Uzbekistan, Tajikistan, Kazakhstan and Xinjiang have fallen off the radar for many in the West, and seem the epitome of remoteness, the opposite is the case. For countless centuries, Kyrgyzstan and the Central Asian region, linking Europe with the Pacific, was literally and figuratively the centre of the world. Passing through it, the Silk Road acted as a bridge between east and west, and prompted the flourishing of civilisations along its length. Today, the whole region again lies at a global crossroads, and there is no better time to get reacquainted with it and to experience Bishkek, one of its biggest cities. Its unique blend of culture, history, religion, language and peoples will live with you forever.

About this guide

Most guidebooks skip over Bishkek or only give the most rudimentary of overviews. This is a shame, as Bishkek has a lot to offer if you just scratch the surface. This guide aims to unearth the city's treasures and fill in this deficit of details. You will get in-depth information on all points of interest, whether buildings, statues, parks, markets or places of worship, researched through personal visits and by drawing on the expertise of locals.

- *Getting to know Bishkek* gives a brief history of the city and examines its history, geography and demographics.
- *Part 1* delves into the two landmark markets of Bishkek, if not the whole of Central Asia, the Osh and Dordoi bazaars.
- *Part 2* takes a close look at Chuy Avenue and its major sights, split into four short walking tours.
- *Part 3* investigates the religious scene in Bishkek and visits some of the most notable churches and mosques.
- *Part 4* takes a break from Bishkek and looks at some of the spectacular hikes on the city's doorstep. It also explores the Burana Tower and the ancient site of

Balasagun.
- ***Part 5*** gives you all the practical information you need to prepare for a trip to Kyrgyzstan.

List of Maps

Here is a list of the maps that feature in this guide:

Map A: Osh Bazaar
 Map B: Western Chuy Avenue
 Map C: Philharmonic Square
 Map D: Ala-too Square
 Map E: Eastern Chuy Avenue

Getting to know Bishkek

A brief history

Bishkek traces its earliest origins back to the time of the Persian-speaking Soghdians, who settled in this region of Central Asia well over a thousand years ago. For many centuries after that, the area where Bishkek now stands remained in relative obscurity as just one of many caravan rest stops strung out along the Silk Road. However, in 1825, the authorities of the Khanate of Khokand, a now-defunct state which used to spread across Kyrgyzstan, Tajikistan, eastern Uzbekistan and southeastern Kazakhstan, decided to fortify the humble caravan stop. The result was a fortress named "Pishpek", and from there they controlled local caravan routes and collected taxes.

The imposition of taxes and other controls by the Khokand Uzbeks naturally caused resentment and hostility among many Kyrgyz, which led some tribes to form alliances with Russia. Others aligned with the Uzbeks, according to clan loyalties. Throughout the middle of the nineteenth-century more and more Russian settlers immigrated to the area, and in 1862 they managed to eventually expel the controlling

Uzbek factions. The fort was completely razed to the ground by the Russians, who then built a new town also named Pishpek on the same site. In 1876, Pishpek and Kyrgyzstan officially became part of the Russian empire. This integration signalled the beginning of a period of mass immigration from Russia, and the newcomers began many large-scale housing, education, mining and infrastructure projects.

After a brief period of independence after the 1917 Bolshevik revolution, Kyrgyzstan became part of the USSR in 1924, with Pishpek as its capital. After the death of the famous Kyrgyz-born Soviet General Mikhail Frunze, the city was renamed Frunze in his honour in 1925. During the Soviet period, Frunze developed into a modern, cosmopolitan city.

After independence in 1991, the government renamed the city as Bishkek. However, many of the Soviet-era buildings still stand proud, and the effects of Soviet town planning are very much in evidence. This has resulted in the city retaining a unique Soviet atmosphere.

Geography

Bishkek is in the far north of Kyrgyzstan a mere 25 km from the border with Kazakhstan. The city rests at an altitude of 800 m on the fringes of the Ala-Too mountain range, an offshoot of the mighty Tian Shans. In contrast to its lofty neighbours, Bishkek lies in the relatively flat Chuy Valley, which extends across the northern half of Kyrgyzstan towards Lake Issyk-Kul in the east.

Central Bishkek is laid out on an easy-to-navigate grid. The main street, running from west to east, is Chuy Avenue, and the most important government buildings, universities, museums, statues and parks are arrayed along this thoroughfare. Other west-east streets of note, running parallel to Chuy Avenue, are Jibek Jolu and Kiev Street. The most prominent road running north to south at right angles to Chuy Avenue is Yusup Abdrahmanov Street, formerly known as Sovietskaya. The road leads all the way to Dordoi Bazaar in the north. Erkindik, or Freedom, Street is another major route, running north from the railway station.

Demographics

Just under one million people live in Bishkek, and of these about two-thirds are Kyrgyz. Sizeable ethnic minorities include the Russians at 9% of the population and Uzbeks at 15%. Others include Tartars, Uighurs, Kazakhs and Ukrainians. Russian is mother tongue for the vast majority of people.

PART 1 - The great markets of Bishkek

— A walk around Osh Bazaar —

Osh Bazaar *(Map A, point 1)* is the ideal place to start any tour of Bishkek. It gives you a glimpse into the everyday lives of Bishkek residents and gets you acquainted with many items unique to Kyrgyz and Central Asian culture.

This vast, sprawling market is one of the most significant and iconic in Central Asia. It's Bishkek's answer to Amazon; it sells just about anything you need, lots that you don't need, and all instantly available at agreeably low prices. As you approach the market you will begin to see vendors selling items from cloths laid out on the pavement, and people selling mobile phone credit, snacks and drinks. However, you will find the main entrance proper on the corner of Kiev Street and B. Beyshenalieva Street.

* * *

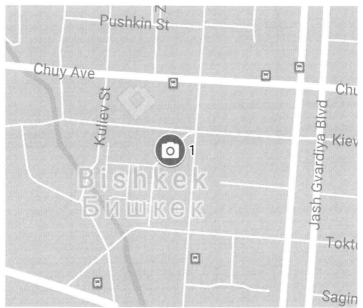

Map A: Location of Osh Bazaar

Once inside, the sheer range of merchandise on offer is overwhelming. However, the stalls are grouped loosely according to what they sell, for the maximum convenience of shoppers ready to bargain hard with the tightly-packed merchants. So, there are zones for clothes, shoes, toys, herbs, dried fruit, fresh fruit and vegetables, meat, rice, electrical goods and much more. It is easy to get lost, so try to keep an eye out for landmarks so that you can keep your bearings.

The experience of visiting Osh Bazaar is one of deep immersion in the Central Asian culture. The crowds comprise native Kyrgyz, Kazakhs, Uzbeks and more. Signage is all in Kyrgyz and Russian Cyrillic, with English characters being a rarity. The vendors are mostly no-nonsense local women, colourfully-dressed and ready to bargain hard. If you know a few Russian words, it will help no end.

City Guide to Bishkek

Keen photographers will have their hands full trying to capture all the colours, sights, people and produce. But don't forget that other sense - taste! Many snack and drinks stalls break up this mass of commerce and provide a perfect opportunity to try all the major Kyrgyz specialities in one place. If you're visiting at breakfast time (or any other time you feel a little peckish), look out for the stalls piled high with the circular loaves of bread called *nan* (or *lepeshka* in Russian), ubiquitous in Osh Bazaar and throughout Kyrgyzstan and Central Asia. It is almost always round in shape and about 30 cm in diameter, and bakers press an ornate design, specific to each region or country, in the middle of each loaf. The bread is baked in a tandoor oven, with the dough slapped roughly onto the oven sides. It's a delicious staple served with every meal.

You're also guaranteed to come across homemade fermented mare's milk, known locally as *kumis*. A staple throughout Kyrgyzstan, it is kept in a bucket or hide container for a few hours or days, and during the fermentation process is stirred now and then to stop it going off. Interestingly, some academics believe that Bishkek takes its name from the paddle that is used to mix the kumis, although others dispute this theory. During fermentation, bacteria make the milk acidic, and yeasts result in the drink becoming slightly carbonated and weakly alcoholic. While the mass-produced kumis you see in glass bottles may use cow's milk, the kumis served directly from the hide at Osh Bazaar will be the real deal. While kumis is an acquired taste, you should at least try a sip or two.

Stalls all around Osh Bazaar sell mountainous piles of *kurut*, a form of salty dried yoghurt sold in balls of various sizes and roughly hewn rock-like lumps. It is made by straining sour milk and yoghurt. The resulting strained liquid is dried and then rolled and formed into various shapes. It is sharply salty with cheesy undertones, and while your taste buds may rebel at first contact, you could get hooked after a few more bites.

Continuing the fermented theme, brewers use fermented grains to produce *maksym*. Its ingredients include fat, flour, water, yeast and barley. It is usually served chilled and is a favourite summer beverage. Similar traditional drinks include *jarma*, *aralash* and *chalap*, and the biggest brand offering all of these is Shoro, which you'll see everywhere around Kyrgyzstan.

There are some reports online of 'fake police' operating within Osh Bazaar, and other dubious practices targeting vulnerable tourists. While this is by no means a widespread occurrence, there's 'no smoke without fire', so an accompanying local tour guide will act as a good deterrent. To be doubly safe, don't take any valuables, wallets and so on, and carry a photocopy of your passport.

— Getting lost in Dordoi Bazaar —

Dordoi Bazaar is one of the biggest, if not *the* biggest, markets in the whole of Asia, and shows that the spirit of the Silk Road is still well and truly alive and flourishing. The statistics surrounding this market are mind-blowing and resemble those of a small country. In fact, Dordoi Bazaar makes an invaluable contribution to the Kyrgyzstan economy. Its turnover is said to be more than USD 3 billion a year and provides both direct and indirect employment opportunities to 150,000 people.

There are two main elements to the market's business model. The first is as a straightforward market serving the needs of locals. Before the market was established just after independence, there were limited retail offerings in the country, and people often went across to Kazakhstan and further afield to buy specific items. Dordoi Bazaar gives these people the convenience of shopping locally. The second, and arguably most important, business for the market is the entrepot trade. Goods from China are shipped over the Torugart pass, into Kyrgyzstan and delivered to the market. There, traders re-export to Kazakhstan, Russia and all over Central Asia, taking full advantage of tariff differences.

Situated at the extreme northern edge of Bishkek, halfway between the city and the Kazakh border, Dordoi Bazaar stretches for well over a kilometre. It is comprised of eight separate markets which over time have grown into each other, and today the boundaries have blurred, so it is hard to see when you leave one market and enter another.

Like a giant Lego set, Dordoi Bazaar is built from thousands of 40-foot shipping containers. Some estimates put the number at 30,000. Stacked in two levels, the lower acts as a shop, and the upper as the storage area. Together, these containers form alleys, streets, squares and the entire structure of the bazaar. As with most markets in Central Asia, the shops cluster together in areas specialising in certain types of products. So there are areas for electronic goods, clothing, kitchenware, toys, furniture, car parts - the list goes on and on. Of particular interest is the section selling winter fur hats and traditional Kyrgyz clothing, including the *kalpak*, the distinctive white felt hat. Fresh produce is absent, although there are many stalls selling snacks and drinks.

Dordoi Bazaar traces its humble beginnings back to 1992, when local businessman Askar Salymbekov initially started the market on a piece of waste ground next to Spartak Stadium just near Panfilov Park. He intended to give traders an area to sell goods that they got on their visits to Kazakhstan and Russia. Demand was so high for space that he bought an abandoned factory site on the edge of Bishkek, and from there Dordoi Bazaar has steadily grown to its current mammoth proportions.

To get to Dordoi Bazaar, take buses 4 or 17 which travel north up Yusup Abdrahmanov Street. Alternatively, many marshrutkas serve the market throughout the day. A taxi will cost about 300 Som one way.

PART 2 - *Exploring Chuy Avenue*

Chuy Avenue is the main thoroughfare of Bishkek, running west to east and splitting the city into two halves of roughly equal size. Tree-lined and pleasantly leafy in the summer, and with beautiful snow covered branches in the winter, this street is home to most of the notable buildings and landmarks of Bishkek.

One relaxed day is enough to tour the whole length of Chuy Avenue and this guide will carve it up into four manageable chunks:

- **Western Chuy Avenue** - from near Osh Bazaar to the Philharmonic Square
- **Around Philharmonic Square**
- **Around Ala-too Square**
- **Eastern Chuy Avenue** - from Ala-Too Square to TsUM department store and Victory Square.

— Western Chuy Avenue —

Starting from Osh Bazaar (map B, point 1), walk one block

north on B. Beyshenalieva Street. Once at the Chuy Avenue junction, walk east. Three and four-storey buildings line this stretch of the street, with shops on the ground floor and apartments above.

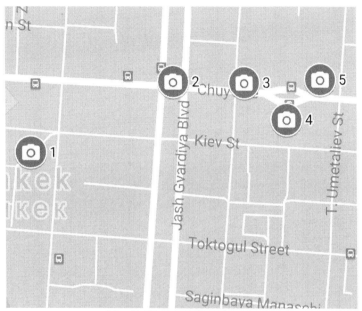

Map B: Western Chuy Avenue

Young Guards Boulevard

After about 300 m, Chuy Avenue intersects Young Guards (Jash Gvardiya) Boulevard. A broad tree-lined park, home to many statues commemorating various Red Army soldiers and war heroes, separates the two one-way streets that comprise this boulevard. At the junction with Chuy Avenue is the Monument to the Heroes of Komsomol *(map B, point 2)*. This distinctive golden statue on a tall granite plinth depicts a young Red Army soldier and a Kyrgyz soldier, together going forth to defeat the enemies of communism. The Konsomol was the youth arm of the communist party, and it aimed to teach youngsters the value of collectivism. Its members showed great bravery in the Russian Civil War and the Second World War, which this monument commemorates.

Kalyk Akyev statue

One block further east from Young Guards Boulevard, diagonally opposite the October Theatre, is a statue of Kalyk Akyev *(map B, point 3)*. Akyev was a Kyrgyz poet and famous Manashi, a narrator of the Epic of Manas. He was born into a family of nomadic cattle herders in the Tian Shan mountains, and from the age of fourteen began to compose songs and poems describing the sad fate of the Kyrgyz people. During the Soviet period, however, his works focused on how the prospects of Kyrgyzstan had been dramatically improved, and of how happy the lives of the people had supposedly become. Akyev was also an accomplished musician, and the statue shows him playing his *komuz*, a Kyrgyz instrument similar to the lute.

Kyrgyz State Academy of Law

A short distance east from the Kalyk Akyev statue, Chuy Avenue splits around a grassy central reservation. At this point is the Kyrgyz State Academy of Law *(map B, point 4)*, a tertiary-level educational institute dedicated to training the next generations of legal professionals in Kyrgyzstan. It's quite a big operation, with 8000 students and more than 200 lecturers split across multiple campuses.

* * *

Zoological Museum

Opposite the Academy of Law is Bishkek's Zoological Museum *(map B, point 5)*. This old-school display of the flora and fauna of Kyrgyzstan, Central Asia and further afield, comprises many cabinets of stuffed birds, animals and fish. For anyone passing by it is worth a peek inside, to get an insight into Kyrgyzstan's natural history. However, there are reports that opening times are sporadic at best, so be prepared.

— Around the Philharmonic —

A couple of blocks further east from the Zoological Museum is the airy open space and park fronting the Philharmonic Hall. This square is a favourite place for Bishkek residents to gather in the summer, surrounded by leafy avenues of trees, bright flower beds and cooling fountains. The square is circled by many other notable buildings.

* * *

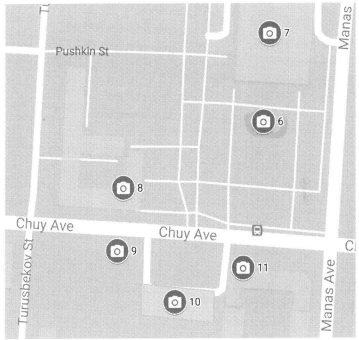

Map C: Around the Philharmonic

Manas the Great statue and sculptural complex

In pride of place, right in the very centre of the square, is a grouping of statuary honouring the main protagonists in the Epic of Manas *(Map C, point 6)*. On the tall plinth is the statue of Manas the Great himself killing a dragon while astraddle his horse. The two smaller figures in front of the central statue depict the wife of Manas, Kanykei, and the sage Bakai.

After spending a few short hours in Bishkek, you will probably already become familiar with the name Manas. You arrive into the country at Manas International Airport. Then, wandering around the city, you will see banks, restaurants, streets, universities and pretty much everything else named after Kyrgyzstan's most famous folk hero.

Manas is the hero of the Epic of Manas, one of the world's most accomplished, yet most overlooked, pieces of literature. While The Iliad and The Odyssey have been studied and read all around the world, the Epic of Manas remains celebrated only in Kyrgyzstan and amongst Turkic speaking peoples. It is undoubtedly an epic, with an estimated half a million lines of verse, thirty times longer than the already weighty Iliad.

To the Kyrgyz, the Epic of Manas represents the spirit of the nation, showcasing its strength in the face of overwhelming adversity. There is some debate as to its age, with some believing it dates back a millennium, while other academics point to similarities with events happening around the sixteenth century. Whatever the truth, one thing is sure - it is a cultural treasure, and Kyrgyzstan holds it close to its heart.

An epic with hundreds of thousands of lines is, of course, impossible to summarise adequately. However, in essence, it is the story of Manas and his descendants, and battles against Khitan and Oirat enemies, from the area of modern-day Mongolia and northeast Asia, form a recurring theme. Manas was the son and only heir of a shepherd and grew to become famed for his strength and leadership. This reputation reached the ears of the Oirat, and a plot is hatched to capture him. When this plan fails, Manas unites his people and becomes Khan. He then goes on to wage victorious battles against the many enemies arrayed around his lands, supported by his faithful warriors and followers.

If you attend one of the many festivals during the summer in Kyrgyzstan, you may hear parts of the epic read by talented narrators called Manaschi. Busts arrayed either side of the Philharmonic square commemorate the most famous ones. Also, if you find yourself in the northwest of the country near Talas, you can visit the Gumbez of Manas, a mausoleum purportedly containing the remains of the great man.

Philharmonic Hall

The Philharmonic Hall *(Map C, point 7)*, built in 1980 is a prime example of a Soviet brutalist concrete structure. Depending on your architectural taste, you'll either love it or loathe it, but it's nonetheless refreshing to see such unchanged Soviet architecture. The hall takes its name from the venerated Kyrgyz composer and musician Toktogul Satylganov. Known mainly as just "Toktogul" throughout the country, much of his work focused on class struggle and accordingly angered Tsarists and the establishment as a whole. As a result, he was sent to Siberia at the end of the nineteenth-century for hard labour. In 1902, he escaped and quickly returned to Kyrgyzstan and wrote many patriotic songs. He was a great supporter of the Russian Revolution and soon turned his attention to composing work lauding communist ideals. His fame and popularity stretched way beyond Kyrgyz borders and across the whole Soviet Union.

The Philharmonic Hall hosts an eclectic range of performances throughout the year, including classical music, ballet, and national folk music. However, it can be difficult to get hold of a programme of events online, so you'll probably instead need to try your luck by going into the box office while in the area. It's on the side of the building facing the university.

International University of Kyrgyzstan
* * *

On the western side of the Philharmonic square, on the corner with Chuy Avenue, is an imposing building with a collonaded facade, topped out by an octagonal tower with a steeple. This houses the International University of Kyrgyzstan *(Map C, point 8)*, founded by the Kyrgyz government in 1993, shortly after the country's independence. To improve medical science in Kyrgyzstan, and to further develop health services for the local population, the International School of Medicine was added to the university in 2003.

Kyrgyz National Bank

A similarly impressive building on the other side of Chuy Avenue from the university is the Kyrgyz National Bank *(Map C, point 9)*, also with extravagant columns and prominent steeple. It was established after independence in 1991 to manage monetary policy, regulate financial institutions and issue money. For visitors interested in the Kyrgyz currency itself, which is quite collectable owing to its rareness, the bank offers some unusual souvenirs in the form of numismatic sets of banknotes, uncut sheets of banknotes, and notes set in acrylic blocks. To buy these, visit the bank's office on 101 Umetaliev Street, just a block away.

Bishkek City Hall

On the south side of the square, facing the Philharmonic Hall, is the Bishkek City Hall *(Map C, point 10)*, with its distinctive collonaded portico with pale blue pediment. This is home to the office of the Bishkek mayor and the local government that administers the city's 170 square kilometres. It manages all essential public services and property, provides emergency services and enforces local laws. The current mayor, elected in 2016, is Albek Sabirbekovich Ibraimov. The turnover of mayors is quite brisk, however, and there have been 13 other mayors preceding this incumbent.

Mineralogical Museum

Next to the City Hall, on the southeast corner of the square, is the Mineralogical Museum *(Map C, point 11)*. It showcases the various rocks, minerals, crystals, geodes and fossils found in the country. Needless to say that a nation classed as 90% mountainous offers geologists a vast array of specimens!

— Ala-Too Square —

Ala-Too Square is the cultural, political and geographical heart of Bishkek. It was built relatively recently, in 1984, to commemorate the 60th anniversary of Kyrgyzstan becoming part of the Soviet Union. Since then, it has played host to many national celebrations, and conversely, in 2005 and 2010 the square was the backdrop to fierce political demonstrations.

Ala-Too means 'great mountain' in Kyrgyz and nicely sums up what the country is all about - its overwhelming mountains. Indeed on a clear day looking south, the snow-capped Tian Shan mountains tower behind the southern end of the square, seemingly within arm's reach. For a walking tour of the area in and around the square, the most obvious starting point is in front of the State History Museum.

Map D: Around Ala-too Square

State History Museum

The imposing bulk of the State History Museum *(Map D, point 12)* dominates the northern end of the Ala-Too square. A textbook example of Soviet architecture, the building was initially purpose-built to contain a museum dedicated to Lenin. Once Kyrgyzstan declared independence, the museum was overhauled to examine Kyrgyz history, from prehistoric times, through the Soviet period to the modern day. Inside, there are apparently some rare Soviet murals with Lenin and communist party imagery. However, the museum is under extensive restoration, and it is unknown whether these will survive. At the time of writing, January 2018, the museum was still closed, but it is slated to open sometime during the year.

Manas the Great Statue

This statue of Manas *(Map D, point 13)* sits directly in front of the State History Museum, and in this depiction the great folk hero is again on horseback. However, the message given by this statue is very different from the one in front of the Philharmonic Hall, which showed Manas with a sword in his hand slaying a dragon. This one is more conciliatory, with Manas' sword firmly sheathed, and hand raised in a friendly greeting. The original sketches for the statue reportedly called for Manas to be brandishing his weapon. However, as the monument was erected to mark the twentieth anniversary of Kyrgyz independence, it was changed to emphasise peace and unity instead. Indeed, the Cyrillic inscription on the plinth translates as 'Magnanimous Manas'.

Interestingly, this site in Ala-Too square has seen a rapid turnover of statues in recent years. Lenin gesticulated proudly from this spot for many, many years, when, in 2003, it was moved to behind the State History Museum for obvious ideological reasons. For around the next ten years, the site housed the Erkindik monument, a statue of liberty featuring a winged woman representing freedom. The government installed the current Manas statue in 2011, but who knows what might appear next?

Monument to Chingiz Aitmatov

Across the street, at the southernmost end of Ala-Too Square, next to Kiev Street, stands the Monument to Chingiz Aitmatov *(Map D, point 14)*. At first glance, you might wonder about the identity of this rather casual looking statue, a man with tie askance and jacket slung carelessly over his shoulder. The inscription on the plinth doesn't help you in this regard, being all in Cyrillic. Don't let this fool you; Chingiz Aitmatov was the most revered of all Kyrgyz writers, to such a degree that he enjoys the same stature that Shakespeare has in England.

He became famous internationally in the 1950s, and his works were translated from Kyrgyz to more than 150 other languages. In the '60s, he switched to writing in Russian, and he eventually earned three state prizes and a Lenin prize. Through his novels and plays, he combined Kyrgyz folk-tales and poetic descriptions of the Central Asia landscape, with more down-to-earth, gritty Russian realism.

If all that wasn't enough, alongside his writing Aitmatov found time for a successful political and diplomatic career. As well as being an advisor to Mikhail Gorbachev and then a member of the newly-formed Kyrgyz parliament, he also acted as the Kyrgyz ambassador to multiple European countries and spent many years in Brussels.

For any first-time visitor to Kyrgyzstan, Aitmatov's most acclaimed work, published in 1958, is highly recommended. Jamila tells the story of a Kyrgyz village girl falling in love with a crippled war veteran, while her husband was away at the front during World War Two. It is set in the northwest of Kyrgyzstan and gives a rich taste of Kyrgyz culture and life during that time, and the collective farming which was then widely practised throughout the country. If there is one Kyrgyz novel that you read, it should be this one.

The Kyrgyz National Flagpole

* * *

Crossing back over Chuy Avenue, on the western side of the square, is an unmissable 45m-high flagpole *(Map D, point 15)* from which flutters a giant national flag. The Kyrgyz flag has a bright red background with a stylised yellow sun in the centre. As with much else in Kyrgyzstan, the flag's symbolism has a strong link to Manas the Great. The predominance of red in the flag derives from the red flag which Manas carried. The Epic of Manas states that the hero united 40 different peoples to create the original Kyrgyz nation, and to mark this achievement the sun has 40 distinct rays. The criss-cross markings on the sun symbolise the straps that secure felt to the frames of yurts, the traditional dwellings of the Kyrgyz people. So taken together, all the elements of the flag speak of heritage, unity, tradition and love for the homeland.

People's Friendship Monument

Back across Chuy avenue, walking west towards the White House, there is a small park, in the centre of which is the grim, 1970's Soviet-style People's Friendship Monument *(Map D, point 16)*. This was erected in 1974 to mark the 100th anniversary of Kyrgyzstan joining the Russian empire. The thirteen figures at the base of the two marble pylons represent the unshakeable friendship between the people's of the two nations.

Monument in honour of those killed in 2002 and 2010

* * *

Continuing towards the White House is a monument *(Map D, point 17)* commemorating those who lost their lives in the protests of 2002 and 2010. It comprises two separate pieces, one white and one black, and in between them, freedom fighters are shown pushing away the darker stone, thus indicating the victory of good over evil.

The 2002 riots broke out in the southern district of Aksy in response to the arrest of a popular local politician, who opposed the then president, Askar Akayev. Local police fired live rounds into the crowd of protestors, resulting in five killed and significantly more shot and wounded.

In the years leading up to 2010, increasing corruption, a weak economy and alleged election fraud all combined to increase the disgruntlement of the Kyrgyz people with the then-president Kurmanbek Bakiyev. The spark for the protests in April 2010 was the government's steep increase in fuel, water and gas prices. Demonstrations quickly spread throughout the country, and the president declared a state of emergency, arresting oppositions leaders and closing down media outlets. Lengthy bloody battles between protesters and security forces around Ala-Too square culminated in the storming of the White House and Parliament, at which point the police started shooting. An estimated 88 demonstrators lost their lives. Bakiyev clung on to power for a few more days, before eventually fleeing into exile in Kazakhstan.

The White House

The White House *(Map D, point 18)* is the office of the President of Kyrgyzstan. It is fronted in white marble, hence the building's name. 'Stalinist Modern' in style, the building has a striking resemblance to others built in Moscow at a similar time, particularly the State Planning Committee building. During the 2010 riots, protestors set part of the building on fire, with many original records and files destroyed.

The Kyrgyz president is the highest office holder in the land. Voters elect presidents for six-year terms. The office was established in 1990 when the transition to independence took place; before then the leader of the country was known as the Chairman of the Supreme Soviet, operating under the auspices of the USSR. The very first elected president was Askar Akayev, and he held office for fifteen years from 1990.

The political transition from a sitting president to a new president has seldom occurred without unrest. The Tulip Revolution ousted Akayev in 2005, and his successor, Kurmanbek Bakiyev was himself overthrown in the 2010 riots. However, the current president, Sooronbay Jeenbekov, did manage to peacefully take over from his predecessor in November 2017.

One of ten children, Jeenbekov was born in Osh. His father was a collective farm manager, and through his early life, Jeenbekov also followed a career in agriculture, becoming a farm chairman. Entering politics in 1993, he became a member of parliament in 1995, and by 2007 had risen through the ranks to become Minister for Agriculture. In the year before being elected as President, he was Prime Minister. In the election, Jeenbekov won a relatively comfortable majority, securing 55% of the votes.

Panfilov Park

Behind the White House is Panfilov Park *(Map D, point 19)*, one of the city's most well-known and visited. It is also known as Red Star Park because when the park's paths were originally laid out in Soviet times, they formed the outline of a communist star when seen from the air.

Ivan Panfilov was a Soviet general who saw distinguished service during the Russian Civil War and First World War. However, it was his success in the Second World War which cemented his position as a Soviet national hero. During this time he commanded the 316th Rifle Division, which primarily consisted of Kyrgyz soldiers. They played a key role in the successful defence of Moscow against the Nazi invaders, and just 28 of their men destroyed 18 German tanks in a display of great bravery. Panfilov was killed during this action. Afterwards, his old division was renamed Panfilovskaya in his honour, and they continued their success against the Germans by taking part in their expulsion from Russia. Across Central Asia and Russia, many districts, parks and streets still carry Panfilov's name.

Today the park is a popular place for families to gather, and children enjoy riding on the ageing fairground rides and eating sweets and snacks from the various vendor stalls. The park also plays host to Panfilov's statue.

Parliament of Kyrgyzstan

Exit the park through the eastern gate, next to the big Ferris wheel, and walk down Abdumomunov Street. After 100 m or so, on the left, is the Kyrgyz Parliament building *(Map D, point 20)*. Unlike governments in some countries, such as the UK and US, who have an upper and lower house of lawmakers, the Kyrgyzstan parliament is unicameral. The single chamber, known as the Supreme Council or Jogorku Kenesh comprises 120 members of parliament, who are elected every five years. As many different political parties hold seats, none of whom have an outright majority, coalitions are created to govern effectively.

Mikhail Frunze Museum

A block north of the Parliament building, on the corner of Razzakov and Frunze Streets, is the Mikhail Frunze Museum *(Map D, point 21)* commemorating the life and works of the man who played a prominent part in the Russian Revolution and subsequent Russian Civil War.

Frunze was born in Bishkek, and in the early 1900s became involved with the Bolshevik movement. He led striking textile workers, and subsequently was arrested and sentenced to life hard labour in Siberian prisons. After ten years he escaped and resumed his revolutionary work through his work as editor of a Bolshevik newspaper. Later in 1917, he led armed forces of workers in the fight for control of Moscow.

As a reward for his valiant role in the revolution, Frunze was appointed a Military Commissar. He eventually took control of the Southern Army group, during which time he led successful campaigns in Crimea and Uzbekistan. Frunze's glittering career culminated in him becoming Chairman of the Revolutionary Military Council, which brought him into direct and sometimes stormy conflict with Stalin. Frunze died shortly after that, and it is still debated today whether Stalin played some nefarious role in his death.

Nevertheless, the city of Bishkek was renamed Frunze in the year after his death and remained so until independence in 1991. This explains why Bishkek airport still retains the rather curious FRU code.

The museum surrounds his old house, and you can walk around rooms packed with old nineteenth-century furniture and personal memorabilia. Information is presented in

Russian only, so to get the most out of the visit a knowledgeable English speaking guide would be preferable.

The museum opens daily, 10 am to 5.30 pm, except on Mondays.

Lenin Statue

Walking back down Razzakov Street to Abdumomunov Street, a rare Lenin statue *(Map D, point 21)* confronts you from across the street, something which has become increasingly rare as time races on from the collapse of the Soviet Union and communism. They used to be ubiquitous throughout the USSR and other communist countries, with Lenin's poses becoming stereotyped into distinct categories: arm or arms outstretched, walking forward purposely, holding a cap, wearing a cap and so on.

Since then, while other countries have toppled most of their Lenin statues, they are still standing relatively proudly in Kyrgyzstan. However, this particular Lenin statue used to be in the most prominent position in Ala-Too square. In 2003 it was replaced by the Erkindik freedom monument and moved to a slightly less conspicuous place behind the State History Museum.

The statue in Bishkek shows Lenin staring out defiantly and standing proud with one arm outstretched. It is clear that the sculptor wanted to show that Lenin was pointing in the direction of a promising future. In front of the statue, there is still a star-shaped flower bed, filled in the summer with bright red flowers. While the country has moved on, this corner of Bishkek is still redolent of the old Soviet times.

— Eastern Chuy Avenue —

From the Lenin Statue, continue along Abdumomunov Street a short distance, and you'll come upon another of Bishkek's expansive green spaces, this time Dubovny (or Oak) Park.

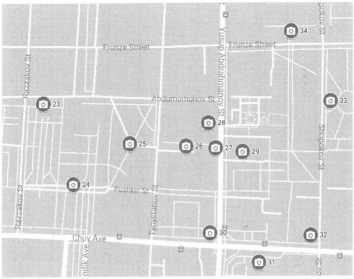

Map E: Eastern Chuy Avenue

Monument to Marx and Engels

At the extreme north-west corner of the park is a monument to Karl Marx and Friedrich Engels *(Map E, point 23)*, the philosophers and revolutionary socialists whose theories, together with those of Lenin, formed the basis for twentieth-century communism throughout much of the world. In this statue, the two bearded and remarkably similar-looking men, wrapped up in warm coats, seem engrossed in their discussions of how to create a working-class utopia!

Statue of Kurmanjan Datka

In a semi-circle of columns at the southern edge of Oak Park, alongside Pushkin Street, is a memorial to Kurmanjan Datka *(Map E, point 24)*. Lenin's statue previously filled this position, and this illustrates the importance of Kurmanjan in the Kyrgyz national psyche.

Kurmanjan Datka, also known as 'The Queen of the South', was a nineteenth-century Kyrgyzstan ruler and stateswoman, and the 2014 Hollywood film 'The Queen of the Mountains' has recently immortalised her epic story. For the Kyrgyz, Kurmanjan embodies the national traits of strength, courage in the face of adversity and independence.

She was born in 1811 in the southern Alai mountains, and at an early age, she was given to a man in an arranged marriage. She rejected him and fled back to her village, something which would still be unthinkable in some parts of Central Asia today. Instead, she decided to marry a nobleman she loved called Alymbek Datka. This insistence on marrying for love is the first reason why Kurmanjan is a Kyrgyz hero, particularly in this case for women.

Her husband was later assassinated, and regional Khans and leaders approved the transition of power to Kurmanjan. At the time, Tsarist forces were expanding throughout Central Asia, and her husband and even sons were involved in the resistance. Kurmanjan, however, realised that such resistance against such a superpower was futile, and persuaded the Kyrgyz people to lay down their arms. Such wisdom saved many lives.

The Russians later captured her oldest son. She did not fight the Russians to save his life, as she realised that this would have such severe repercussions for the country. This heroic selflessness made it clear to the people that she would not sacrifice their wellbeing to save just one of her offspring.

Today, the Kyrgyz still revere Kurmanjan Datka, and you can even see her image on the 50 Som banknote.

Memorial to the Red Guards

In the northeastern corner of Oak Park is a red granite obelisk *(Map E, point 25)*, surrounded by bronze cannons, which pays tribute to the forty-three Red Guards who died during the 1918 anti-Bolshevik Belovodsk Uprising. Still proudly topped off with the hammer and sickle, the inscription on the obelisk reads "Eternal glory to those who died for the power of the Soviet".

The uprising was led by one of the parties fighting the revolution in the Russian Civil War and was a revolt by peasants in Belovodsk protesting the policy of prodrazvyorstka, whereby authorities requisitioned agricultural produce from peasants at a low fixed price. The uprising went on to threaten Bishkek, and so the Red Guards under the leadership of Logvinenko were dispatched to put out the fire of rebellion. After a few days Bishkek was secured, Belovodsk recaptured and calm restored. Logvinenko survived the action, and after his death was also interred at this site, alongside his comrades-in-arms.

Cholponbek Bazarbaev statue

Across Tynystanov Street from the Red Guards memorial stands a statue dedicated to Cholponbek Bazarbaev *(Map E, point 26)*, the top ballet dancer and actor of the Kyrgyz Opera and Ballet Theatre. He spent more than 20 years of his life as an active part of the national ballet troupe, before eventually becoming the CEO of the theatre, which looms in the background. He was tragically killed in a car accident in 2002, and this statue commemorates his contribution to the Kyrgyzstan cultural scene and the art of ballet.

Aaly Tokombaev

Just behind Cholpon Bazarbaev is another statue, this time dedicated to the famous Kyrgyz poet, composer and novelist Aaly Tokombaev *(Map E, point 27)*. He wrote poem collections focusing on socialist ideologies and the struggle against Tsarism and won many Soviet honours including the Order of Lenin. He made one of the most significant contributions to Kyrgyz literature.

Fine Arts Museum

Next to the statue of Aaly Tokombaev is the imposing concrete bulk of the Gapar Aitiev Fine Arts Museum *(Map E, point 28)*. Don't let the grey, forbidding and ramshackle exterior put you off; inside there are many outstanding artworks from both Kyrgyz and Soviet artists. There are many styles on offer here from traditional oil paintings of Kyrgyzstan scenery, and Soviet renderings of peasantry at work in fields, through to modern art, photography and sculpture. So there should be something for everyone. Of particular interest to foreign visitors is the ground floor display of traditional handicrafts including intricate carpets and beautiful felt work.

The museum takes its name from Gapar Aitiev, the first national artist of Kyrgyzstan. He became famous for his landscapes and depictions of agriculture. Many of his paintings feature farmers and labourers close up in the foreground, while the majestic mountain scenery unfolds in the background. Some of his work is on display in the museum.

The museum is open daily, 10 am to 6 pm, except on Sundays and Mondays.

State Opera and Ballet Theatre

Home to the Kyrgyz national ballet and opera, the elegant State Opera and Ballet Theatre building *(Map E, point 29)* stages a wide range of performances throughout the year, and also hosts some visiting shows. Prices are low by Western standards, although it is important to note that most operas are in Russian, so maybe the ballet is a better option if you do not speak that language. As there is no website, the easiest way to find out about productions is to go and read the advertisements posted on the front of the building.

Monument to Fighters of the Revolution

On a large site on the corner of Yusup Abdrahmanov Street and Chuy Avenue is the Monument to Fighters of the Revolution *(Map E, point 30)*. Turgunbai Sadykov sculpted it, the artist also responsible for many other statues around Bishkek including Manas the Great outside the Philharmonic Hall and the Friendship monument next to the White House.

The woman with a flag in her hand, representing revolution and social freedom, gestures to two smaller statues of freedom fighters and pays tribute to their ultimate sacrifice.

Kyrgyz Telecom Building

Standing tall over the Kyrgyz Telecom building is a monumental clock tower *(Map E, point 31)*, perhaps Bishkek's answer to Big Ben. It's yet another example of Soviet 1970s-style architecture and is worth a look when in the area.

TsUM Centre

On the corner of Chuy Avenue and Shopokov Street is the TsUM Centre *(Map E, point 32)*. TsUM stores can be found all over Russia with the most famous example being the one in Moscow on Theatre Square. The name TsUM is an acronym standing for Tsentralnyi Universalnyi Magazin, or Central Universal Store, and true to its name, the five-story department store seems to sell just about everything. The layout is curiously old-fashioned, with merchandise sold from many independent stalls, grouped on each floor according to the category of goods on offer. The ground floor is a maze of mobile phone stores, with seemingly endless variety on offer. In the basement, mobile phones can be taken for repair. Other levels focus on clothing, electrics, household items and more. Of interest to visitors, the top floor sells a wide range of souvenirs, and one can negotiate prices to very reasonable levels.

* * *

Victory Square

Continuing 200 m north past TsUM on Shopokov Street, you reach Victory Square *(Map E, point 33)*. This expansive square was built in 1984 to commemorate the fortieth anniversary of the victory against the Nazis in the Second World War (referred to as the Great Patriotic War in Russia and ex-USSR states). Although Kyrgyzstan was a long way from the front, this by no means reduced the impact on the country. It sent 360,000 men to fight, and 160,000 of these did not return. Every town, village and hamlet lost someone. As a result, such monuments can be found all over the country.

Victory Square is dominated by the Monument to Victory at its very centre. The monument's three granite arches represent the shape of a yurt, the traditional Kyrgyz dwelling. At its peak, you can see the same criss-cross markings as those used on the national flag, and these are the straps that are used to hold the felt of the yurt together, and thus evoke unity. Under the arch is a statue of a Kyrgyz mother, awaiting the return of her sons and husband from the front. An eternal flame also burns at this spot.

There are two other accompanying statues in the area of the monument. The first features two men dissembling a machine gun, and the second shows a group of men returning from war accompanied by their children.

The monument is a favourite backdrop for the wedding pictures of Kyrgyz newlyweds, and on the weekends it is common to see one wedding party after another line up under the arches for their photos.

Kyrgyz State Circus
* * *

Stephen Stocks

From the northern end of Victory Square, the surreal outline of the Kyrgyz National Circus building *(Map E, point 34)* is just across Frunze Street. A prime example of socialist modern architecture, completed in 1976, the structure resembles a recently landed flying saucer.

Circuses are a popular form of entertainment in Russia and the ex-Soviet Republics, and this one still stages shows regularly. Depending on your views on performing animals, you may prefer to admire the building just from the outside.

PART 3 - Places of worship

Mechet Imeni Mahmud Kashgari mosque

Kyrgyzstan has an overwhelmingly Muslim population, with more than 85% of people being followers of Islam. Since independence, there has been a revival of interest in the religion, and new mosques have been built around the city, often through donations by wealthy Gulf states.

A beautiful example of one of these new mosques is the Mechet Imeni Mahmud Kashgari mosque. From Victory Square, go east along Frunze Street for 600 m, then turn right onto Osmonkul Street where you can find the mosque. With its golden domes, four striking minarets and intricately decorated facades, the mosque took three years to build and opened in 2017. It takes its name from Mahmud Kashgari, the eleventh-century Islamic scholar.

Holy Resurrection Cathedral

Slightly more than 10% of Kyrgyzstan practices Orthodox Christianity, and most of these come from the Russian community. Orthodoxy was first introduced into the country when it became part of the Russian Empire in the nineteenth-century, and the first churches were opened to provide places of worship to Russian soldiers building forts.

One of the most iconic orthodox churches in Bishkek is the Holy Resurrection Cathedral on the corner of Jibek Jolu Avenue and Togolok Moldo Street, in the area north of Panfilov Park and Spartak Stadium. From the outside, it is typically Russian Orthodox, with golden onion domes, whitewashed walls and blue spires. Inside there are no pews as you'd see in Protestant or Catholic churches, and worshippers stand throughout their devotions. Icons cover the walls and altar screen, and candles burn on golden candelabra. Black-robed priests conduct services at around nine in the morning and six in the evening when you can hear beautiful chanting and singing.

Church of the Holy Prince Vladimir

This new Russian Orthodox Church is now touted as the biggest in all of Central Asia and can accommodate 2500 worshippers at a time. It opened in 2015 to mark the 1000th anniversary of St Vladimir the Great, the Kievan ruler who introduced Christianity into Russia.

The church soars to 34 m in height, topped with a giant golden onion dome with an oversized cross. Inside, as with other Orthodox churches, there are no pews but instead standing space for the worshippers. A choir sings from the balcony during some services, and if you are lucky, you may hear a choir practice session.

The church is a bit out of the way on the extreme southern fringe of Bishkek on Aaly Tokombaev Street, near the American University of Central Asia. However, you will probably pass it on the way back from Ala Archa. Visitors should take care not to photograph the church, as the on-site security guards strictly forbid it.

PART 4 - Day trips out of Bishkek

— A day out hiking in Ala Archa —

Ala Archa is a spectacular gorge less than an hour's drive south of the capital. It offers some of the best scenery in the country, and by being so close to Bishkek, visitors can get the full alpine experience for which Kyrgyzstan is famous, yet without the expense and effort of going to more remote regions. Its clear mountain air also provides a much-needed respite from the city which can get dusty and hazy during summer months. The park contains twenty glaciers, fifty mountains and numerous streams and rivers; accordingly, it is very popular among hikers, picnickers, horse riders, skiers, climbers and just about anyone who loves the great outdoors.

Along the bottom of the gorge runs the fast flowing Ala Archa river. As much of the river is glacial meltwater, it has a strange milky white colour, caused by tiny rock particles created as the glacier erodes the valley floor and sides. The water is pure, however, and of course icy cold. Up the slopes of the surrounding mountains run fir and juniper trees (archa) from which the valley and river get their name. The juniper has traditionally been held in high esteem by the

Kyrgyz, and they burn its branches to ward off evil spirits. In the summer, many other alpine plants and flowers speckle the slopes. Wildlife that might be spotted includes the wild goat, roe deer, wild boar and eagles. Much rarer, at the higher levels, is the snow leopard.

The park entrance is about a 25 km drive south from Bishkek. At this point, there is a barrier across the road, where you need to pay the entrance fee for each visitor (80 Som) and a vehicle entrance fee if you are in a taxi. If you are travelling by marshrutka, you need number 265 from B. Beyshenaliyeva Street near Osh Bazaar; however these will go no further than the checkpoint, and as the trailhead is a further 12 km down the road, you will have to walk or hitchhike the rest of the way.

At the trailhead, there is the Alpager, a small cluster of buildings including an A-frame alpine style guest house, at an altitude of 2000 m. In the summer there are usually a few yurts dotted about with some touristy activities on offer for visitors. It is at this point that the main hiking trails begin.

Waterfall and Ratsek base camp hike

This hike is the most popular option from the Alpager, although probably the most strenuous. Having said that, anyone with a reasonable level of fitness can manage it. The primary objective is to reach the Ak-Sai waterfall, which cascades around 30 m down the mountainside. While the falls themselves are relatively diminutive compared with more famous counterparts, the views are spectacular. The Ak Sai Glacier is visible in the distance.

From the Alpager, follow the path on the left signposted Ak Sai, which wends its way steeply up the valley side through thick forests of fir. Eventually, you will climb above the tree line from where you can get awe-inspiring views of the Ala Archa river. After about an hour, you reach a dramatic outcrop of rock looking out over the confluence of the Ala Archa with the Ak Sai river, and this provides a much-needed excuse for a rest. The trail continues along the Ak Sai river until it reaches the waterfall after another couple of hours. In total, the path is 3.75 km long and climbs 700 m in altitude, which is more than enough exercise for most visitors.

For more serious hikers, the trail continues up significantly steeper and more rugged terrain for another three hours to the Ratsek base camp at the base of the Ak Sai glacier at the height of 3350 m. An overnight stay would be necessary before returning down. For mountain climbers, this camp is just the starting point, with many other high peaks up to 5000 m.

Ala Archa river hike

A well-marked trail meanders along the bottom of the gorge next to the Ala Archa river. The path extends for more than 10 km on relatively level ground. From the Alpager, go straight all the way past the start of the waterfall trail. You can decide to turn around any time you wish depending on how your legs feel, but many visitors aim to go the 10 km to the entrance of the Top Karagai valley before returning. For more adventurous climbers, it is possible to ascend this side valley all the way up to the Top Karagai glacier at the height of 3680 m.

Andigene valley and glacier hike
* * *

This trail starts a few hundred metres back down the road from the Alpager. It begins by following the Ala Archa river before angling steeply up the west side of the gorge through a larch tree forest. The path then goes along the beautiful Andigene valley replete with waterfalls, forests and rivers stocked with many trout. Along the way, there is a cemetery containing the graves of mountaineers who perished on the surrounding peaks. The trail eventually comes to an end after 8 km at the Andigene glacier at an altitude of 3300 m.

Be prepared

The peak season for hiking in the Ala Archa runs from May to October. While it is possible to walk in the winter months, extreme weather can make this dangerous and inadvisable.

Even in the summer, you need to be careful. It can be sweltering hot in the city, but when you get up to the Alpager, it may be cold, wet or windy. Even if the weather is cooperating when you start walking, conditions can change rapidly in the mountains. Therefore it is best to be prepared. Carry a day pack with some warm clothing, wet weather gear, water and some snacks. A mobile phone would be a good idea too.

If you prefer to visit Ala Archa with someone who knows the ropes, the Trekking Union of Kyrgyzstan (www.tuk.kg) offers a wide range of day hikes with experienced guides.

— A day out hiking in Alamedin Valley —

Alamedin is the second biggest gorge after Ala Archa, and the scenery is just as dramatic. It is a similar distance away from Bishkek as Ala Archa, at around 30 km to the south-east of the city. The good news is that there is no entry fee. Also, as most tourists have Ala Archa on their 'to-do' lists, Alamedin is quieter and more frequented by locals rather than foreign visitors.

Where the road from Bishkek ends at the Alamedin trailhead, there is an old Soviet swimming pool filled with water from nearby hot springs. The water gushing out from the bowels of the mountain is at 56C, and the swimming pool maintains a constant 30C. It is full of minerals such as calcium, magnesium and iron, and is said to cure a range of musculoskeletal and neurological diseases.

The hiking trail starts just after the bathhouse and runs alongside the Alamedin river. The terrain is flatter and more comfortable to traverse than that of the Ala Archa gorge, making this hike suitable for people of all fitness levels. Children would also enjoy the walk. The valley bottom is quite broad and covered in birch trees, juniper, pussy willow, and wild fruit bushes in the summer. These alpine meadows are surrounded on either side by spectacular 4000 m plus peaks, topped out by a variety of glaciers.

Most visitors walk for about an hour and a half, to a point where the valley widens out near its junction with the Salyk valley. On the left side, clear mountain springs can be seen, with water bubbling out from under the rocks. There is a beautiful 12 m high waterfall cascading down the mountainside a little bit further up this Salyk valley. In the winter this freezes into a surreal ice sculpture comprising many giant icicles.

— A day trip along the Chuy Valley to Burana

—

Once out of the eastern industrial suburbs of Bishkek, the road to Burana parallels the Kazakh border, just a couple of kilometres away in some places. The countryside here in the Chuy Valley is very fertile, and rich arable fields stretch away in all directions.

The easiest way, albeit the most expensive option, is to book a private car and driver to take you there. The journey will take about an hour and a half each way from the city centre. The cheaper alternative is to get a marshrutka or bus number 353 from Bishkek East bus station to Tokmok, and then hire a taxi from Tokmok to the tower site. Finally, Bishkek and Tokmok are linked by railway, although the train is very slow taking two hours, and its late afternoon timing makes it an impractical option.

Kant

By road, the first town to be reached after Bishkek is Kant. Some think that this small town was named after the German philosopher, as it played host to thousands of Germans forcibly relocated here from Russia during the Second World War. The reality is more prosaic, however, as the Kyrgyz word for 'sugar' is Kant, with the town taking its name from a sugar mill opened there in the 1930s. Today Kant is also home to a busy air base currently being used by the Russian Air Force.

Tokmok
* * *

The next major population centre is Tokmok, nestled just inside the border with Kazakhstan. It is here the road branches off to the Burana Tower site. While the town is not of interest to the passing visitor, keep an eye out for the remarkable Ilyushin Il-28 fighter-bomber plane mounted on one of the roundabouts in an otherwise nondescript residential area.

The Burana Tower

The Burana Tower is the remains of a minaret, which would have been part of a much more extensive mosque complex. The minaret initially stood at about 50 m, but an earthquake in the fifteenth-century toppled the upper half, so reducing the height to the current 25 m. The octagonal base and circular tower are built entirely from bricks. A modern staircase gives access to the minaret. Once inside there is a dark and extremely steep, winding staircase which goes all the way to the top platform, from which there are spectacular views across the Chuy Valley to the snow-capped Tien Shan mountain range. When going back down, it is advisable to go backwards.

Burana Tower is a listed as a UNESCO World Heritage Site.

A brief history of Burana Tower

Burana Tower is one of the most prominent remains of Balasagun, an ancient city originally founded by the Persian-speaking Soghdians. Balasugun is almost unheard of outside Kyrgyzstan, yet it played a pivotal role in the development of the Silk Road. In its heyday, it was considered to be the actual centre of the world.

In the tenth-century, the Karakhanids came to power in Central Asia and displaced the earlier Soghdian settlers. Their Khanate became the largest and most powerful state in the region and stretched across what is now much of Uzbekistan, Tajikistan, southern Kazakhstan and parts of Kyrgyzstan. Other major urban centres included Samarkand and Kashgar, but Balasagun had the distinction of being the overall capital city. The Karakhanids were a Turkic people and were strong adherents to Islam. They ensured that the religion had a solid foothold throughout the region, from which it spread and flourished.

In the thirteenth-century, Mongol armies invaded Balasagun and brought an end to the Khanate. Unusually, the city was spared and was left mostly intact. However, after the invasion, the importance of Balasagun gradually declined, and after a century or two fell into ruin.

Legends

Many legends swirl around the tower, and one of those most-repeated involves the story of a local king and his daughter. Upon the daughter's birth, a witch had warned the king that she would die by the age of eighteen. The understandably worried king wanted to protect his daughter and prevent this predicted death, so he built the tower and installed her at the very top. No one entered the tower except the king and a servant which who brought her food. On her eighteenth birthday, when all appeared as if the prophecy would not come true, the food the servant took up contained a poisonous spider. The daughter was duly bitten and died, as the witch had predicted all along.

* * *

Stephen Stocks

Hidden treasures

Archeological investigation of the site has literally only scratched the surface, and there are possibly many other treasures to be uncovered with many lumps and bumps in the area around the tower indicating buried buildings. The most prominent of these is a 100 m x 100 m mound directly alongside the tower, which experts believe could hide the remains of a palace or temple complex. We won't know the answer until more funding becomes available to start excavation.

Balbals

Scattered around the Burana Tower are dozens of balbal grave markers. Balbal is the Turkic word for ancestor or grandfather, and these carved obelisks mostly have a likeness of a face engraved upon them. The ones around Burana Tower date from the sixth to eighth centuries, although balbals have been discovered elsewhere that date back another 1000 or so years. Balbals are found all over Central Asia, and these examples come from sites all over Kyrgyzstan.

Petroglyphs

Also surrounding the tower, nearby the field of balbals, is a collection of petroglyphs, giving an insight into the lives of the very earliest inhabitants of Kyrgyzstan. These are stone drawings made centuries before Christ and can be more properly described as inscriptions as they were created by scratching a smaller sharper stone over the larger rock to form the picture. Most images are of animals that these early residents would have hunted, such as deer, wild boar, horses, sheep and camels. As with the balbals, archaeologists gathered these examples from around the country.

Museum and gift shop

There is a small onsite museum which displays a few artefacts discovered around the tower during archaeological work. The Burana Tower ticket price includes museum entry. Next to the museum is a yurt which houses a gift shop selling souvenirs, and some books giving more details on the long history of Balasagun.

The entry fee for Burana Tower and all the other displays mentioned above is 50 Som.

PART 5 - Preparing for your visit

— Essential info —

When to visit

Kyrgyzstan has a continental climate, with cold winters and hot summers. However, due to the extreme mountainous character of the country, weather also depends on elevation.

Spring and autumn are cool and rainy. During the winter the average temperature is well below zero. The summer season from May to September is preferable, as it is relatively dry, warm and sunny and most of the tourist infrastructure is up and running during these months.

Visas

Kyrgyzstan has a relatively relaxed visa regime, making it a popular first destination for visitors planning a more extensive Central Asian itinerary. Bishkek makes a pleasant base while applying for visas at the embassies of neighbouring countries.

Citizens of 45 countries do not require a visa at all, including most western European countries, Gulf states, Australia, New Zealand, Japan, Korea and Singapore. An additional 20 nationalities can get a visa on arrival at Manas International Airport. For all other nationalities, it is necessary to apply for a visa in advance at a Kyrgyz embassy.

Currency

The currency is the Kyrgyzstani Som (KGS). At the time of writing, January 2018, one US Dollar bought 68 Som, one British Pound bought 98 Som, and one Euro got 85 Som. These main currencies are easily exchanged in the city. A particularly convenient place to change money is on Yusup Abdrahmanov Street, near its junction with Bokonbayev Street. Just about every shop is a currency exchange, and such high competition for customers assures you a reasonable rate.

Time Zone

Bishkek is in the Kyrgyzstan Time (KGT) zone, which is GMT+6. The country does not observe daylight savings time.

Electricity

Kyrgyzstan's electricity is of the 200V/50Hz variety. The wall sockets take plugs with two round pins.

* * *

Languages

The two official languages spoken are Kyrgyz and Russian. While English is spoken well in top-end and mid-range hotels, and by some tour companies, it is less frequently-used on the street, so learning a few words of Russian could come in handy.

— Getting There and Away —

By Air

Bishkek has one airport serving all international and Kyrgyz airlines. Manas International Airport is about a 25 km drive north of the city centre, very near to the Kazakhstan border.

The majority of flights arriving at the airport originate in Russia, or ex-Soviet republics. For visitors coming from Europe or the Middle East, transits in Istanbul, Dubai or Moscow would be the most convenient and comfortable options.

Here are the airlines currently connecting **international destinations** with Bishkek:

- Aeroflot has daily flights to Moscow, with onward connections on its services and those of the SkyTeam Alliance. www.aeroflot.com
- Air Astana flies to Almaty and Astana. www.airastana.com
- Air Kyrgyzstan, with flights to Urumqi, Krasnoyarsk, Surgut, Chelyabinsk, Krasnodar,

Belgograd and Moscow. www.air.kg
- Air Manas, with service to Delhi, Urumqi, Tashkent and Moscow. www.airmanas.com
- Avia Traffic offers the widest selection of destinations from Bishkek, including Jalalabad, Dushanbe, Istanbul, Irkutsk, Krasnoyarsk, Almaty, Novosibirsk, Surgut, Moscow, Yekaterinburg, Kazan, Grozny, Krasnodar, Voronezh and St. Petersburg. www.aero.kg
- China Southern flies to Urumqi. www.csair.com
- FlyDubai offers five times weekly flights to its Dubai hub, with onward connections around the Middle East, Africa, the Subcontinent, the Caucasus and Europe. www.flydubai.com. Alternatively, passengers can connect to Emirates' global network.
- Pegasus Airlines goes to the secondary Istanbul airport, Sabiha Gokcen, with onward connections throughout Europe. www.flypgs.com
- S7 flies to Novosibirsk. www.s7.ru
- Silkway Airlines links Bishkek to Urumqi. www.silkwayairlines.com
- Tajik Air flies to the Tajik capital Dushanbe
- Turkish Airlines has a flight from Istanbul to Ulan Baatar which stops in Bishkek. You can book either leg. From its Istanbul hub, you can fly just about anywhere in the world. www.turkishairlines.com
- Ural Airlines flies to Domedodovo and Zhukovsky airports in Moscow, and Yekaterinburg. www.uralairlines.com
- Uzbekistan Airlines links Tashkent to Bishkek. www.uzairways.com

Due to the mountainous nature of Kyrgyzstan, there are not too many airports around the country. However, frequent flights do connect the **domestic** destination of Osh with Bishkek. Airlines operating this route include Air Kyrgyzstan, Air Manas and Avia Traffic.

By Rail

The topography of Kyrgyzstan does not allow an extensive railway network, and tracks run along the widest and flattest land. The primary international link is the Moscow to Bishkek railway, which transits Kazakhstan. The journey takes about three days. This makes possible an adventurous, albeit lengthy, trip to Bishkek from any railway station in Europe via Moscow, a trip which would take at least one week.

In summer months, a train runs from Bishkek to Lake Issyk-Kul, a journey of about six hours.

By Road

The most straightforward route is from Almaty in Kazakhstan. You can make the entire journey by marshrutka or by hiring a taxi. Alternatively, as Bishkek is very near the Kazakh frontier, you can just get the marshrutka or taxi to the border, and then use readily-available local public transport for the last leg. The complete journey from Almaty to the Kyrgyz border takes three to four hours and the last hop from there to Bishkek about an hour. The immigration processing time can vary according to the time of the day, with the evening rush hour being particularly busy.

* * *

— Getting Around —

From the airport

Many of the longer-haul flights arriving at Manas International Airport land in the dead hours of the early morning. So there are no public transport options available. Upon exiting the baggage hall, there is an intimidating scrum of taxi drivers, all keen on overcharging bleary-eyed tourists who haven't yet grasped the currency. For this reason, it is better to invest in an airport pick up organised by your hotel or guest house. You will then be guaranteed a stress-free entry into Kyrgyzstan.

After spending a few days in the country, you should have met some friendlier taxi drivers, and you can arrange a return transfer for around USD 10.

Around the city

Like many other places in the ex-Soviet Union, Bishkek has an extensive marshrutka network. These are fourteen-seater minibuses which usually cram in many more people standing up. You can flag down a marshrutka anywhere on the side of the street, and its number and ultimate destination is marked on the windscreen. Similarly, you can also get off anywhere along its predetermined route. A ride costs 10 Som. The public transport website for Bishkek, www.bus.kg, details all the services and routes. It has an easy-to-use map interface; just click your start and end points, and the full list of marshrutkas is displayed.

The city also has a more conventional bus network, with buses stopping at designated bus stops only. The same www.bus.kg website also displays all the route information.

Finally, you will see taxis cruising everywhere around Bishkek, and you can easily hail one from the street. To book a taxi, call the three-digit telephone numbers of private taxi firms, such as 150, 152, 154 and 156. You can usually negotiate a half or full day hire with the driver for a reasonable rate.

— Where to stay —

Bishkek may be off the beaten track, but there are many comfortable options at all levels. Here are just a few highlights in the top end and mid-range categories, however www.booking.com lists all the possible options at the competitive rates. Furthermore, Tripadvisor.com compares prices with the three or four top hotel consolidators, making sure you get the most reasonable rate. There is also a wide selection of apartments and rooms to rent in Bishkek on www.airbnb.com.

Top end

The Hyatt Regency Bishkek is the all-bells-and-whistles luxury hotel in Bishkek. Centrally located on Yusup Abdrahmanov Street opposite the Fine Art Museum, the hotel is within an easy walking distance of all the major sights. There is an outdoor swimming pool and a good selection of restaurants and bars.

The Ambassador Hotel is down a quiet side street off Moskovskaya Street, near the Ala-Too square. Rooms are spacious and well appointed, and the hotel provides a luxury experience while being excellent value for money.

Orion Hotel is a highly rated 5-star hotel in a business district on Erkindik Avenue. It offers a super indoor swimming pool, and all public areas and guest rooms are lavishly appointed.

Jannat Regency is a bit further out on the southern fringes of the city. While the hotel is aimed squarely at business travellers, it is also a good choice for families, as guest rooms are outsized, and there is a large outdoor swimming pool and children's play area.

Golden Tulip is a firm favourite among regular visitors to Bishkek, offering all the facilities you'd expect from an established global hospitality brand. It is a few minutes walk away from the Bishkek Park shopping mall.

Mid-range

Futuro Hotel is a quirkily-designed, European-budget style hotel, offering free breakfast and two-way transfers to and from the airport or the Kazakh border. You need to book rooms early as the hotel is usually booked well in advance.

Solutel is next door to the Ambassador Hotel and is owned and managed by the same company. Consistently given great reviews, the hotel is in a quiet area, home to many embassies, yet just a couple of blocks away from Chuy Avenue.

City Hotel Bishkek is a reasonably-priced option around 3 km, or a 10-minute drive, south of the centre, on Baitak Baatyr Street.

* * *

Smart Hotel is also on Baitak Baatyr Street, albeit a kilometre or so closer to the centre. Rated for its modern, spacious rooms, and free airport transfer.

My Hotel is just off Chuy Avenue, about a kilometre east of the TsUM department store. The newly-opened hotel offers fantastic rates and a good selection of supermarkets, cafes and exchanges surround it.

Copyright

FewDaysAway

PO Box 215878
   Dubai
   United Arab Emirates

www.fewdaysaway.com

This edition published 2018.

Copyright (c) Stephen Stocks 2018